Tantrums!

Managing Meltdowns
in Public and Private

Thomas W. Phelan, Ph.D.

ParentMagic, Inc.
Glen Ellyn, Illinois
www.123Magic.com

Illustrations by Rex Bohn
Graphic Design by Mary Navolio
Distributed by Independent Publishers Group

Printed in the United States of America
10 9 8 7 6 5 4 3 2

For more information, contact:
ParentMagic, Inc.
800 Roosevelt Road, B309
Glen Ellyn, Illinois 60137

Library of Congress Control Number: 2014907466

Contents

You're Not Alone!

As upsetting as they can be, and as difficult as they are to manage, young kids' **temper tantrums are usually simply a primitive response to good parenting.** These loud and sometimes violent outbursts of anger do not mean you've done anything wrong as a parent or caretaker. Instead, temper tantrums most often mean that you are doing your job. And a difficult job it is! See if any of this sounds familiar ...

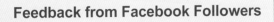

Feedback from Facebook Followers

Q: Your kid's into a total nuclear meltdown. What's the most difficult part of that for you?

Not losing my cool. Mom is tired and frustrated too, but I don't get to kick and scream. Sara N.

Keeping your calm and ignoring, especially when it goes on for a long time. Jill F.

Mine's not even 5 yet, but I think she has learned this one through the "divatude" in public because at home you know you can't get away with it. Barkshire W.

Glad I'm not alone. I fear my own inability to keep cool and not allow myself to get to his level. I have days where I feel like the crappiest parent. Karen S.

Dealing with the noise, which is annoying. Controlling the urge to try to reason with them at the moment. Sibyla S.

For me it's the sound of the scream/cry!! I usually do well with not giving in, but I don't want to lose control and scream/cry back at them. Ashley F.

Keeping my cool. The feeling that rises up is a mixture of anxiety and anger, and the desperate need to control the situation. Channa B.

Feedback from Facebook Followers

Q: How do you feel about managing children's tantrums in public?

I struggle with being in public. All parents most likely have "been there," however as the mother of a tantruming child you can't help but feel the stares and judgments being passed to you when you are carrying the child out of the room/store, etc. Jill F.

I must agree with some of the others about children-with-an-audience tantrums. They learn that parents don't want to be embarrassed and the kids push buttons in front of an audience sometimes. Barkshire W.

Tantrums don't really bug me, except that I'm embarrassed that people are seeing/hearing my kid that's totally out of control. I worry that I'm being judged. Heidi D.

Afraid of DCFS!!! Far too many nosey people ... You barely raise your voice above a whisper and they call it "child abuse". Shauna N.

Parents are afraid other people will report them for "abusing" their kids. I know it's the first thing that comes to my mind when I have to stand outside a business for a time-out with my kid bellowing. LaCosta L.

Feedback from Facebook Followers

Q: **How long does it take to recover from a youngster's major meltdown? For the kid, maybe seven minutes. For the parent, three hours.**

So true!! I'm so glad it's in writing too, so I don't feel like it's just my problem. Katie V.

No wonder my day goes to crap with only three fits. Angie S.

Or longer, for the parent! Julie A.

Glad to see I'm not the only one who feels exhausted after dealing with meltdowns. Grzenzia M.

My little boy's meltdowns do me in for the day. Ella J.

Q: **When your child is having a blow up after not getting something they wanted, how effective is reasoning and explaining?**

I equal this to them hearing me as the teacher in "Peanuts." They can't hear words at that point. It's just noise. Tara L.

You cannot reason with a child that is already tantruming. Diane S.

If she doesn't get the point when she's CALM, how on earth will she grasp it during a screaming/crying/kicking FIT? Although, I would actually say the fact that she is throwing a tantrum means she DOES understand, but refuses to accept my decision. So she tries to change the answer with the fit. Allison Z.

About as bad as trying to reason with an out-of-control adult. But you do have a better chance—you are the adult. Cheryl H.

Feedback from Facebook Followers

Q: How does your child's meltdown affect your feelings about yourself as a parent?

Useless, knowing I did something to put her in a situation that led to her meltdown and unsure how to help her. They're getting more violent and destructive now. Feel helpless most of the time. Corinne K.

Terrible. Like a total failure. Deborah M.

It affects me negatively. Even though I know it isn't really my "fault," it frustrates me that it happens. I feel embarrassed that I haven't been able to teach self-control. Fraser B.

Fine. Tantrums aren't allowed in the rest of the house. Keep that business in your bedroom. Now, if the kids are hurt or sad, I'd love to snuggle. Tantrums, though, they gotta work out on their own. Sarah Q.

Depends on what the tantrum is about. Personally if I am doing everything right then all is good. If your kid has a meltdown, let them. Angela P.

It doesn't really. I take them at face value and try not to read into them. She's 2. If she's not throwing tantrums I'm doing something wrong. Melissa J.

Lately, his tantrums make me feel like I've failed, especially in public as I have a very defiant, over-reactive, loud 5-year-old who I've got no way to connect with once he gets in that mood. Vanessa R.

In this book we'll get you ready to manage your youngster's tantrums more effectively, both in public and in private. You're going to learn some surprising things. In addition to understanding that a child's tantrum is not your "fault," you're going to learn that what you need to do in managing meltdowns is often the exact opposite of what you feel like doing. From now on, when your kid blows, you're going to know how to stay in control!

Three Terrible Tantrums

Of all the behavioral problems parents face from their children, temper tantrums may be the most upsetting as well as the hardest to manage. A major temper tantrum might also be the most potent tool kids have when it comes to *training their parents to do what the children want*. Parents who have been trained to fear tantrums have an extremely difficult time maintaining control of their own homes.

A lollipop at 6:30 a.m.?

Good parents are both warm and demanding. That means they can't give their youngsters everything the kids want. Here's a little girl who would very much like a sucker for breakfast. When she realizes Mom has a different food choice for her, she *energetically* makes her feelings known. She also puts her poor mother in an early morning quandary.

To bed or not to bed?

Here's another little one who doesn't want to do something his parents want him to do: Go to bed and stay there. He's fine until they leave the room. Looks like a long evening ahead for Mom and Dad! A super-agitated child is not going to nod off very quickly, and these parents are going to pay for their "insensitivity."

How about a little Angry Birds?

Another common source of tantrums is a child wanting to start an activity his caretakers think he should not. In the mind of this seven-year old, Angry Birds trumps dinner. Mother's demand that her son do dinner first is met with resistance, which then generates a *really silly "conversation"* between Mom and boy. The frustrating dialogue leads directly to the youngster's outburst.

Outcomes of tantrums

None of the outcomes of tantrums is particularly good. If parents can't stand the noise, they may give in. This reinforces the child's outburst and also lets the youngster have something or do something that is not good for him. On the other hand, *parents who can't stand the noise may produce a tantrum of their own,* by either physically spanking or beating the child or by attempting to out-scream their little one. Repeated episodes of this kind are a major stress to other family members. Poorly managed tantrums can cause extreme marital strife as well as chronic depression.

- **Parent capitulates/reinforces**

- **Parent is emotionally or physically abusive**

- **Spoiled brat, marital stress, parental depression**

A very unpleasant way to live!

For many adults, the absolute worst part of a kid's tantrum is the tantrum itself. The noise, the drama and the anguish on the part of the child can produce a horribly painful combination of rage and panic in the parent—especially when the tantrum occurs in public.

On the one hand, the parent is scared that he or she won't be able to end the outburst any time soon. On the other hand, the stricken adult becomes enraged at what they see as the extreme, unnecessary, embarrassing and irrational behavior of their offspring.

This rage/panic combination results in what is akin to a state of temporary insanity which 1) is extremely painful and 2) makes it *very difficult to think and act clearly.* And as time goes by, for many parents just the threat of a tantrum can produce this same anxious and befuddled mental condition.

Panic + Anger
=
Temporary Insanity!

That's the problem and that's the bad news. Is there any good news? Yes, but managing tantrums involves some hard thinking and some hard work. Sure, you'd like to come up with some strategy for eliminating tantrums altogether. Believe it or not, some of you will actually be able to quickly accomplish that objective. But most of you probably won't be so lucky so fast. Most of you will have to first learn how to manage tantrums well, then you need to stubbornly stick to your new strategies while you watch your children's outbursts gradually *decrease in frequency, intensity and duration.* Some of you will get good results in just a few days, others of you will have to go through "Hell Week," in which the kids get worse before they get better.

3 Big Lessons

How are we going to accomplish this feat? We first need to examine how most parents think about tantrums, and how that thinking needs to be changed. *This means a major Attitude Adjustment.* You can't do what's right unless you're thinking clearly about a problem. We're also going to analyze exactly how the process of a tantrum works—including your reaction to it.

1. What To Think *(Attitude Adjustment)*

2. What To Do *(Battle Plan)*

3. What If? *(Troubleshooting)*

Our attitude adjustment and tantrum analysis will point us directly to our solution. It will define our Battle Plan. What To Think leads straight to What To Do. You will learn what your options are when you are faced with a tantrum—or the threat of a tantrum. You'll learn how to remain calm and decisive, as well as how to make up your mind quickly in the heat of battle. And, as you'll find out when we discuss our 10-Second Rule, you don't have a lot of time to decide how to respond to an upset youngster.

Finally, and before you start doing anything differently, we'll troubleshoot our solution for your situation. Since kids can immediately "smell" weakness as opposed to resolve in their parents and other caretakers, it's important that you understand and anticipate all the problems that might arise when you start managing things in new ways. This "What If?" analysis will help temper the steel inside you, letting your kids know that you mean business.

What we need from you …

Some programs simply present you with new information and then wish you luck. But for this program, *Tantrums!*, to work, *we need something from you*. First of all, sometimes you're going to have to be very supportive and understanding of yourself. Why? Because there are going to be times when doing the right thing is going to make you feel worse first. That's the way it goes with tantrums. Second, we need you to master the concepts described here thoroughly, then do the job well. Half-hearted attempts won't work—in fact, they may make things worse—and there will be times when you will have to act courageously. But when you think about it, in a lot of ways you really don't have any choice.

1. **Supportive of yourself:** Kind and sympathetic— tantrums are a tough problem!

2. **Demanding of yourself:** Master basic concepts and do the job well.

Hold on to your seat, here we go! We've got to start with reasonable thinking—otherwise known as *brutal honesty.*

Lesson I: What To Think

Chapter 1

Attitude Adjustment

First, let's look at what we parents actually think during one of our children's tantrums. Then let's take a look at what we should think—in other words, are there other ideas that make more sense? Then we'll extend our analysis by examining how temper tantrums work. Why do kids behave like this? What are they trying to accomplish? What does a kid's tantrum do to the average parent? It's a tough problem, but you'll soon see that our analysis will point us directly toward the solution.

What parents think during tantrums

Here's what parents often think when their child explodes. The tantrum plus this kind of thinking produces a horrible feeling in an adult.

"OMG, this should not be happening!"

"What did I do wrong?!"

"Is this kid nuts or what?!"

"What should I do? I'm an idiot!"

All these thoughts are incorrect. They are irrational and they have to be abandoned before mom or dad or grandma or boyfriend or babysitter can ever consider handling a tantrum properly. Why?

Erroneous thinking produces three results, ALL BAD

1. **Bewilderment and confusion**
2. **Emotional agitation**
3. **Lousy strategy**

Obviously, a big attitude adjustment is necessary!

What you should think during a tantrum

None of us ever had any training in how to manage a kid's meltdowns. That means agony for adults when kids decide to blow up, and big-time confusion about what to do.

No one in state of mental anguish is going to be able to solve any problem well. And children are automatic experts in being able to read their parents moods, thoughts and behavior. *If kids think that an adult is upset and has no idea what to do, the door opens for that child to play that adult like a violin.*

That's why it's essential that we rethink the series of rapid, spontaneous thoughts that we parents entertain when our children are tantruming. Let's examine each one separately.

"OMG, this should not be happening!"

Percentages of kids with daily tantrums

- 1-year-olds: 14%

- 2 to 3-year-olds: 20%

- 4-year-olds: 11%

- 5 to 6-year-olds: 5%

- 18 to 65-year-olds: ??

OH GOOD! TANTRUMS ARE NORMAL!

OH NO, THEY ~~MAY~~ WILL CONTINUE!!

This tantrum should not be happening? Wrong. Meltdowns, though obnoxious, are normal and common. You cannot wish them away. Tantrums are especially common in one-to-four-year-olds. Many parents get a steady diet of them from their children. Tantrums do not mean your child is mentally ill.

What did I do wrong?!"

Aggravating as they can be, tantrums are often simply a child's primitive reaction to good parenting.

Tantrums have 3 main causes:

1. Not getting a **thing** *(Lollipop)*

2. Having to do an **activity** *(Going to bed)*

3. Not getting an **activity** *(Angry Birds)*

Temper tantrums are usually a simple, normal reaction to simple, good parenting. As well as being warm, affectionate and friendly, good parents OFTEN have to be demanding. That means they can't give their kids everything the youngsters want. Since they are just little people and *don't have a lot of emotional control,* small children often overreact to the frustrations their parents and other caretakers impose. No, you can't have the lollipop for breakfast, yes, you do have to go to bed, and yes, it is time to stop playing Angry Birds. Though these events may seem like major tragedies to the kids right at the moment, in a short time they will have forgotten the whole thing. Their parents, however, may still be shaking from the blow-up.

"Is this kid nuts or what?!"

Tantrums occur spontaneously in normal children who are frustrated. Tantrums have two main goals:

1. Kids want to get their way.

2. Kids want to get revenge if you don't give them their way.

Tantrum behavior can kick in very naturally at an early age, and it has nothing to do with intelligence.

Meltdowns by themselves are not a sign that a child is mentally ill. Even if the tantrums occur many times a day or occur frequently after a child is over five, we still can't determine that a youngster has an emotional or behavioral problem. We have to first train caretakers in good meltdown management, go through a training/trial period, then see what we have left.

Rather than being chaotic signs of a total lack of discipline, tantrums are actually very goal-directed activities. Tantrums can have two goals, and understanding what these goals are is extremely important to managing them. The first goal of a tantrum is for a child to get his or her way. I want the lollipop; I don't want to go to bed; I do want to play Angry Birds and not eat dinner. A tantrum represents a tremendous investment of energy in attempting to get what one wants.

The second goal of a tantrum is one you may not like to hear, but it's just a normal part of human nature. *If you don't give me what I want, Mom and Dad, you're going to get it!* I will make you pay. I am going to make you suffer for being so unreasonably demanding. I may hit you, bite you, throw things or try to make you deaf with my screams.

Chaos? No. Intense, goal-directed behavior.

"What should I do? I'm an idiot!"

With the right attitude and perspective, a good battle plan and the willingness to persevere, I can minimize or even eliminate tantrums.

No one trained us in dealing with kids' outbursts. So naturally, we do feel helpless and ineffective. And when children know we feel that way, it makes the tantrum worse. Our little ones sense that they might get their way if they persist, and even if they don't get their way, the adult's obvious agony lets the kids know that they are effectively punishing Mom or Dad for their insensitivity.

This analysis provides some hints for tantrum management. *We need to rethink how we adults reward tantrum behavior* (and its two goals). Our Battle Plan will have to take this reality into account.

Most of the time kids are very likeable. Tantrums are aggravating and often extremely embarrassing, but they are not the end of the world. I have to learn how to forgive my child for just being a kid. And just think how nice it will be when I can reduce the frequency of—or even eliminate—the tantrums!

FACT Summary

- **Meltdowns are normal.**
- **You did nothing wrong.**
- **Your kid is not crazy— he is goal-directed.**
- **You can and will change this.**
- **Tantrums are aggravating but not terrible.**

So here's our critical Attitude Adjustment. This and the Anatomy of a Tantrum (coming up) will provide the essential basis for our strategy for dealing with the problem. All these ideas are important, but the first two may be the most critical to remember. **First, meltdowns are normal**—they are not a sign that anything is wrong. You may get a steady diet of them while your children are little.

Second, although it seems to feel this way, a child's tantrum is NOT a sign that you did something wrong. On the contrary, you probably did something right (the demanding side of the parenting equation)!

Take a moment to let those two ideas sink in. How will they affect the way you react from now on to a youngster's explosions?

Chapter 2

The Anatomy of a Tantrum

You've now started looking at tantrums differently. Now let's analyze a typical tantrum and see what's going on. You can think of a tantrum as having three possible stages or phases: Veto, Incubation and Explosion. The actual meltdown or explosion is the third stage, and it will not occur unless it is preceded by one or both of the other two.

1. The Veto:
   Their wish vs. your wish

2. Incubation:
   Mutual irritation grows

3. Explosion
   BLAM!

The Veto

Let's examine the Angry Birds example we introduced in the beginning of the program. Remember that tantrums have three main causes that are all based on parent/child conflict. Here the conflict is based on an activity the boy wants but that Mom does not want to allow because of the closeness to dinner time.

> "Can I play Angry Birds on your iPad?"
> *"No, dear."*
> "Why not?"
> **"We're eating in ten minutes."**
>
> **The Veto**

During the Veto phase, the groundwork is laid for the parent/child conflict and ultimately for the child's tantrum—if matters get that far. During the Veto phase, the adult indicates to the child that *the adult's desire is going to supercede the child's wish*. The child is not going to get what he wants. There will be no Angry Birds before dinner.

So the potential battle line is drawn and *the child has a choice: cooperate or file a protest.* It would be nice if children were always capable of saying to themselves, "OK, fine. Better luck next time," and then walk away. Some kids, in fact, will grumble first but then cooperate. This positive reaction is more likely the older a child is. Kids who cooperate are learning what is known as "frustration tolerance" and that's one of life's most important skills.

But other children will push the adult. In other words, the children file a protest against the Veto. By complaining, grumbling or whining, they tell the parent, "I'm going to fight this!" If the youngster files a protest, the process potentially—but not for sure—enters the next phase, tantrum Incubation. Just as the child had to choose between cooperation and protest, now the parent has a big choice to make.

Incubation

If the youngster files a protest, tantrum development may proceed to its next phase: the Incubation stage. What's the parent's choice here? It's *whether or not to participate in tantrum Incubation by means of reasoning,* pleading, whimpering or ineffective attempts at distraction.

Sometimes the Incubation stage determines whether or not a tantrum will occur at all. At other times, as with our lollipop girl, the Incubation stage takes almost no time whatsoever. The meltdown comes right on the heels of the frustration from the Veto. When Incubation does occur, the process involves a rapid, sensitive and highly volatile interaction during which parent and child repeatedly react and counter-react to each other. When this interaction process is negative—and especially when a parent is upset and doesn't know what to do—the likelihood of an angry explosion from the boy or girl becomes greater and greater.

Here's the Incubation stage in the Angry Birds story:

"Oh, come on. Just for five minutes."
"Read my lips. I said 'No'!"
"You never let me do anything!"   **Incubation**
"What!? We just got back from the pool!"

The boy files his protest when he says, "Oh come on, just for five minutes." He puts his parent on notice that he is going to fight the Veto.

What is this parent's strategy for dealing with the son's protest? *It is to engage in a ridiculous conversation.* During the ridiculous conversation, anger escalates on both sides, leading directly to the boy's explosion. Without the silly dialogue, the boy might not have blown up! "We just got back from the pool!" is a true statement that is at the same time useless, silly and provocative.

It is important to realize that the Incubation stage is often very short and sometimes even non-existent. It may be a split second or the Incubation discussion may go on for a few minutes. Since kids can go from calm to explosive very quickly, a general rule of thumb is this: After the Veto (the basic conflict is established and the child has protested), if a *parent can't come up with an effective strategy in ten seconds* or so, the chances of a meltdown become greater and greater.

Explosion

So in some situations kids go straight from the Veto to Explosion. The parents walk out of the bedroom, for example, and their two-year-old explodes immediately. At other times, the children melt down after a silly dialogue. That is the case with our Angry Birds fellow:

| "That's stupid! I hate you!!" | EXPLOSION |

No parent likes to be called "stupid" or to have her kids say they hate her. Older kids may be less physical, and may instead accuse you of being a bad parent, swear or threaten to do awful things. Small children may throw themselves down on the ground, kick ferociously, scream and bang their heads.

A full-blown meltdown in a child makes most of us parents extremely uncomfortable. We want to scream or at least talk to our youngsters to try to pound some sense into their heads, but that usually makes matter worse. It's an awful feeling! Let's look more closely at this state of temporary insanity in our brains.

Chapter 3

The B.A.D. Syndrome

The experience of a tantruming child—or sometimes just the thought of that—can produce something very "bad" in a parent or other child caretaker. That something is a painful and dysfunctional state of mind that we call the B.A.D. Syndrome.

The B.A.D. Syndrome in adults

When faced with a tantruming child, many adults are first bewildered and surprised. Even if they have been through these outbursts many times before, lots of moms and dads still seem caught off guard. This B.A.D. feeling is the opposite of accepting tantrums as normal, unpleasant and repetitive.

- **B**ewildered:
  Surprised—no idea what to do.

- **A**gitated:
  Upset—want to end crisis ASAP!

- **D**efaults to:
  Reasoning as the chief strategy.

WHIMPERING OR PLEADING

B.A.D. SYNDROME

Being caught off-guard also means being at a loss for what to do. All this leads to severe emotional agitation—now the adult is about as upset as the kid is. Because this B.A.D. feeling is very painful, the parent wants to end the crisis as soon as possible. What to do? Oddly enough, many if not most adults in this situation default to reasoning with the child. *Default is the perfect word here*, since adults just seem to fall backwards into talking, pleading and otherwise trying to persuade the child to calm down.

Adult whimpering

To the frustrated child, however, adult reasoning comes across as whimpering. Whimpering at a child during the Incubation stage is like cutting your own throat.

Child immediately smells weakness in

Whimpering

and eats parent alive.

Tantrum escalates

Whimpering is deadly because kids immediately smell weakness in the adult's tone of voice. *To the little ones it sounds as though the adults don't really know what they're doing.* And the little ones are correct!! So the tantrum gets worse. Why does an upset, weak and whimpering adult make the tantrum worse? It's really simple.

The whole B.A.D. Syndrome in an adult gives the child HOPE. Hope for what? Hope that one or both of the goals of meltdowns might be met. If these adults really don't know what to do and if, furthermore, they're really upset, the child thinks, there's a good chance I'll either get my way or I'll at least get them back for not giving me what I want. In other words, indecision and agitation in the adult tell the child that "It's time to go for the gold!"

Pleading
from the adult produces

HOPE

in the child!

1. Maybe I'll get my way!

2. Even if I don't get my way, I'll get revenge.

By the way, this manipulation or maneuvering (or whatever you want to call it) on the part of the child requires no particular intelligence or brainpower. It just seems to come naturally, even in kids under two years of age.

High vs. Low Frustration Tolerance

Each one of these parent/child episodes (and how the parents handle it) is really important for the child's growing up and their ability to mature. Why is that? It has to do with something called "Frustration Tolerance."

There are two lessons all kids have to learn as they grow up:

1) You can't always get your way.

2) It's really OK if you don't get your way all the time.

But some people learn these lessons better than others. Some folks learn to accept frustrations more or less gracefully, not punish those who frustrate them, and move on. Others learn to feel that they should get their way all the time and that not getting their way is unjust or tragic. *They learn to believe that this injustice should be punished.* We used to refer to children like this as brats. Now, with our modern psychiatric sophistication, we call them Oppositional Defiant Disorder (ODD) kids. These kids are emotional (and sometimes physical) bullies and they do not have bright futures.

That's why the Incubation stage is so important. It's at that point that children repeatedly practice one of two points of view. Some kids learn to accept frustration (including limits from authority) as normal, repetitive and transient. You can't get everything you want, that's OK and you move on with life. This is called HFT—*high frustration tolerance*. Other kids whose parents don't handle the Incubation stage well, however, learn to view all frustrations as unjustifiable tragedies. These kids learn LFT (*low frustration tolerance*) and they also come to believe that adults who impose restrictions on them should be punished.

The 10-Second Rule

So when an adult is faced with a child's tantrum (Explosion stage) or with the threat of a tantrum (Incubation stage), it's critical for that adult to respond calmly, decisively and quickly.

After a PROTEST is filed, you have 10 seconds to STOP pleading and to decide what to do.

Ten seconds is not a lot of time. Kids can blow up in less time than that. Useless attempts at reasoning or distraction can lead to (or Incubate) a 50-minute screaming match between you and your child. This increases the chances that the child will either 1) get his way or 2) at least get effective revenge. Those are not skills you want your youngsters to learn. *Time is of the essence!* By whimpering you make the situation right now worse and you make your child's future worse.

So after the Veto and after the child has filed their protest, you have ten seconds to decide whether or not you want to participate in Tantrum Incubation by engaging in a silly conversation.

The B.A.D. Syndrome and not having a strategy for tantrums also mean the next few years are going to be worse for you. B.A.D. means the tantrum problem you are having now will show the characteristics below. And your child will be more at risk for developing ODD.

B.A.D. reinforcement promotes:

1. **More** tantrums

2. **More** violent tantrums

3. **Longer** tantrums

4. **More** years of tantrums

So, in a sense, the bad news is this. You have a short window of opportunity to make up your mind before you start making things worse.

The Good News

But here's the good news. Our B.A.D. analysis points us directly to the outlines of a solution. It won't be easy, but we can at least start to define exactly what needs to be done.

B.A.D. Points to Solutions!

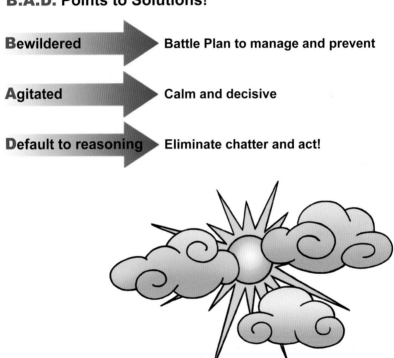

Bewildered → **Battle Plan to manage and prevent**

Agitated → **Calm and decisive**

Default to reasoning → **Eliminate chatter and act!**

Let's Get This Right!

A SUMMARY OF LESSON I

These are all examples of requests. Sometimes requests go from child to parent, sometimes they go the other way around.

This little girl wants a thing.

This boy wants an activity.

This dad wants his son to go to sleep (activity).

Person-to-person requests are an ordinary part of family life. When it's "request time," you need to put your thinking cap on!

This parent is exercising her Veto power.
Vetoes are basically good things, because you
can't give your kids everything they want.

As shown here, this is a good parental Veto.
Good Vetoes have three characteristics:

A. They are short.
B. They offer one explanation if needed.
C. They are followed by parental silence.

These children are "filing their protests"
against parental Vetoes.
At this particular time they do not want to cooperate.

A child's protest can be
simply a little grumbling,
or it can be a full-fledged
meltdown. Kids' protests are
irritating but normal.

These parents are ruining perfectly good Vetoes by whimpering, reasoning and angry chatter.

Whimpering

Angry Chatter

Reasoning

Adult babbling is a good way to incubate, trigger or prolong a meltdown.

These are tantrums. Though they are very commonplace, they can be extremely unpleasant to listen to. Yuck!

Are these kids out of control?
Are they totally sick?
Not at all.

They are very focused on their goal!

Lesson 2: What To Do

Chapter 4

Boot Camp

Now that you understand what tantrums are all about, it's time for us to start talking about how to manage them. You'll need to remember everything we just talked about because that knowledge will help determine your strategy.

Managing a child's tantrums can be a gut-wrenching experience. Why? Because you are often torn into two conflicting pieces. One part of you, for example, wants to give the kid what she wants just to put an end to the noise and to your feeling of temporary insanity. Another part of you, however, realizes that *giving in will only reinforce future tantrums* and make them more likely. That's why it's a good idea to have a Battle Plan in mind before trouble starts.

Two unpleasant facts

Here's what makes dealing with meltdowns so difficult:

1. Usually the only way to STOP a tantrum immediately is to give the child what he or she wants.

Worst thing to do **>** Feels best

2. On the other hand, sometimes

Best thing to do **>** Feels worst

Having a plan before trouble breaks out is essential, but in order to do what's best for you and your youngster, you're also going to need guts. Courage is required, especially in public where it feels like everyone is watching your every move. Remember to be nice to yourself (you didn't invent the parenting job!) and also work hard to do what's right. Also keep in mind that, unfortunately, when you prevent a tantrum successfully or manage a meltdown well, the only person who's likely to give you a pat on the back is you. Your child is certainly not going to provide you with positive feedback!

What about distraction and reasoning?

One other thing has to be mentioned here before we start. Distraction and reasoning are often put forward as tactics for dealing with temper tantrums, but these "tactics" often cause more trouble than they're worth. Why? Because kids—especially as they get older—know what you're up to. *Too often distraction and reasoning are nothing more than parental whimpering.*

Here's the deal. There's nothing wrong with distraction or reasoning if they work. So next time there's trouble, try one or the other or both. But do this consciously—don't default to either strategy. Say to yourself, "I'm going to try distraction" or "I'm going to try reasoning." Then watch what happens. Does it work? If so, great. If not, consider the strategies we're about to discuss.

Think realistically

You can't give your kids everything they want. They can't have everything they want and they can't do everything they want. And to make matters worse, sometimes you have to ask them to do things (like get out of bed or brush their teeth) that they just don't feel like doing. That's your job and it's normal for kids to protest (even with tantrums) when they don't like what you're asking of them.

A tantrum is most often a normal response to good parenting.

Be calm and decisive

When kids warm up for a tantrum or actually explode, they can sense in a split second how you're reacting to their protest and how likely you are to give in. They also know right away how much pain they're causing you or, in other words, how successful they are in achieving revenge.

Remember: Kids can smell your resolve.

Do not default to reasoning

Reasoning is no longer an option in the pinch for you, unless you can prove to yourself from your own experience that logic produces good results. "When upset, open mouth" is not good advice, no matter what you've read in some parenting books.

Talking is so natural, and so destructive!

Chapter 5

The Battle Plan

"I'm not opening that cash register and that's it. You can have all the Tootsie Rolls you want, but you're not getting my cash!"

Ready for action? Your Battle Plan basically has four simple steps to it. The plan doesn't take a lot of thought, but it does take some practice. But how do you know exactly when it's time to put your Battle Plan Thinking Cap on?

You know when it's *request time!* The picture above is based on a true story. A potential robber pulled out a knife and confronted a 95-year-old grocery store owner with this request: "I want all the money in your cash register!" The quote is how she responded. Talk about resolve! The young felon-to-be knew he had met his match and ran out of the store.

Kids' requests at your house are not so dramatic, but they can mean trouble is coming. "Can I have a cupcake?" is a request for a thing. "Can I go outside and play?" is a request for an activity. These wishes come from the kids. They should warn you that it's time to start THINKING because trouble may be BREWING. Your strategy and resolve are about to be tested.

The other kind of request that can set off a tantrum is a request from you, such as "I want you to get ready for bed."

Action instead of talk

Here's the battle plan:

You have two choices before a child files a protest or explodes.

You have two choices after a child files a protest or explodes.

Request time means it's time to get yourself ready for potential trouble. Trouble will occur if you don't give your child the thing they want or don't grant them the activity they want, or if you continue to insist that they comply with your request. Relax and remain calm.

Let's think this thing through. The first two options in your Battle Plan are geared toward preventing meltdowns. These options won't always be successful, but they will help a lot to minimize the frequency of tantrums.

The second two options are more geared toward managing meltdowns or protests after they occur.

Before they protest or explode:

1. Give them what they want.

- **Bad mood Vetoes/requests**
- **Mixed Vetoes/requests**
- **Fatigue, hunger, illness**

First of all, consider whether or not you can let the child have his way. Maybe he can have the cupcake or maybe he can go outside and play. Perhaps you don't have to ask him to get ready for bed yet. Just because this is the kid's third request for something or other, give the matter a little thought rather than simply providing an impulsive "No!"

Obviously, if you give the child what he wants, there will be no further difficulties. Problem solved!

So that's step one: Give the kid what he wants if you can. What if you can't or really don't want to? That will take you to step two of the Battle Plan. We'll get to that in just a moment.

Let's apply step one to the three examples of meltdowns we looked at to begin the book. Can these parents give the kids what they want?

Lollipop: The answer is No. Sorry, young lady. Few parents want their children to have candy for breakfast.

Angry Birds: Yes, these parents could let their son play Angry Birds before dinner if they wished. There's enough time.

Bedtime: Here's another No. This little boy has to go to bed sooner or later.

Before they protest or explode:

2. Lock down your Veto and stop talking.

- ▪ **Brief**
- ▪ **Firm**
- ▪ **One explanation if necessary**
- ▪ **Silence**

It's a good idea to make up your mind fairly quickly regarding a child's request. Be careful with "negotiation"! Too often negotiation becomes badgering on the child's part and simply whimpering on the parents part. If you're going to give the kids what they want, do it in step one. Don't be badgered into it.

Calmly state your decision (can you feel the protest or even explosion coming?). Take a deep breath, give one explanation if necessary (usually it is not necessary), then stop talking. You've done all you can for now. Saying "no" and closing that door early without a lot of hassle is one of the best ways to prevent a meltdown.

What do you do now? You pause and wait.

In our three tantrum examples, how might the parents finalize the Vetoes?

Lollipop: "No, baby. Finish your pancakes and then we have to leave for school."

Angry Birds: "No, dear. We're eating in ten minutes."

Bedtime: "Good night, honey."

These are all nice, firm and friendly comments. But they all mean "No." However, they don't mean "No" if the parents keep talking or chattering. Further chatter will sound like pleading to the children and then you're into the B.A.D. Syndrome.

After locking down your Veto, you are going to let them decide if they want to file a protest (including melting down) or cooperate.

After they protest or explode:

3. Check out (disengage) in 10 seconds.

Imagine you are now confronted with either a mild protest (grumbling, eye rolling, stomping, crying) or a full-fledged meltdown. Now what do you do? Your veto is final.

- **You will do the opposite of what you feel like doing.**

- **You will not talk or chatter.**

- **Your disengagement will be a big surprise to your kids!**

What do you feel like doing? Naturally, *you feel like talking* (or pounding) some sense into their head. Maybe a few firm—or even angry—words will get them to understand. Why can't they take no for an answer? Is it really such a big deal?

Yes, it is a big deal to them and YOU are TOTALLY on the WRONG track if you think like this. Be honest, how many times in the past has talking, persuading or arguing done any good in these situations.? Zero? On the other hand, how often has talking, persuading or arguing made things worse (like in tantrum incubation)? 100%?

GENTLY
CHECK OUT
and leave them alone.

How do you check out?

You decide how to check out

- **Minimal or no eye contact**
- **No verbal communication**
- **Increase physical distance**
- **Walk away or turn your back**
- **Lock yourself in bathroom**
- **Put on headphones**
- **Call yourself on phone**
- **Keep cooking dinner**
- **Other...**

You know yourself and your kids better than we do, so it's best for you to decide how you break off contact. And sure, safety is also an issue. But here are some ways that parents in the past have success-fully checked out or disengaged. The most important ingredients for a successful disengagement are probably no talking, increasing physi-cal distance or simply exiting the scene when possible. Be creative! Going into another room, pushing the grocery cart backwards and locking yourself in the bathroom are entertaining options.

Why do you check out?
Audience / Target / Power

Think about it: Your presence feeds a child's tantrum in three impor-tant ways. First, *you are the audience* that is supposed to appreciate the child's suffering. Second, *you are the target* for the anger/revenge mo-tive that arises from their frustration. And third, *you have the power* to grant or not grant their wish, so you are the focus of their persuasive efforts. Take yourself out of the picture and what have you done? You have removed all the motives for their outburst.

Sure it's easier said than done, but—once again—what's your resolve? And is talking a real option? Some kids will quiet down themselves when you check out. Others will pursue you.

After they protest or explode:

4. Consequence their behavior.

There's no law that says you have to consequence tantrums. Often ignoring/disengaging is enough. But what if the youngster breaks stuff, follows you around screaming, hurts someone else or uses really foul language? In these cases, your message might change to this: Watch your step, buddy, or in addition to not getting what you want, something worse is going to happen to you.

- **Often your just checking out is the best penalty.**
- **Tantrums are for the room**
- **Your screaming or lecturing is a reward, not a consequence.**

Little kids can be moved to cribs, Pack 'n' Plays, rooms or whatever. That movement is both a penalty as well as a disengagement. Let them scream it out on their own. Get your ear plugs or earphones.

A bigger child who is tantruming is probably not going to voluntarily go to a rest period or time-out. So use time-out alternatives.

You may wonder: If I'm supposed to be disengaged and not talking, how do I inform my kid about a consequence? He's already out of his mind to begin with!! You can consider several things. First, you can calmly inform a child about a consequence—once. This will not be a two-way conversation; if you get no good response, so be it. Second, you can have a prior agreement—for every minute they tantrum, for example, they lose 10 cents off their allowance or so many minutes off phone, iPad or video games. Third, you can use counting from *1-2-3 Magic.*

Chapter 6
Our Terrible Tantrums

L et's take our four-step Battle Plan and apply it to the tantrums examples we discussed earlier. Remember, when it's Request Time, 1) give them what they want or 2) finalize the Veto and stop talking. These are your preventive measures. If the child blows up or protests, it's on to 3) gently check out and 4) consequence their behavior. These are your meltdown management measures.

Lollipop at 6:30 a.m.? Anatomy

"Lollipop?" Three-year old asks sweetly.

"No, baby. Finish your pancakes then we have to leave for school." ◄ The Veto

"Lollipop, lollipop, lollipop!" Child throws herself down on floor screaming. ◄ Filing the protest & explosion

"Come on, honey. Help Mommy. We have to leave in 5 minutes." ◄ Whimpering

Kitchen fills with horrible screams. ◄ Explosion worse

The lollipop request starts this ball rolling. Mom does not want to give her daughter candy for breakfast, so she finalizes the Veto pretty well with "No, baby. Finish your pancakes then we have to leave for school." This statement does not prevent the meltdown, however, it actually triggers it. The filing of the child's protest is her explosion. Mom whimpers with her weak "Come on, honey. Help Mommy" statement and, as you'd expect with whimpering, the tantrum gets worse.

Lollipop What to do

- **Cause of tantrum:** child wants material thing
- **Can parent give child what she wants?** No.
- **Veto:** *No, baby. Finish your pancakes."*
- **Child files protest/explodes:** "Lollipop, lollipop, lollipop!"
- **Mom checks out immediately.** Leaves room.
- **Consequence the behavior?** No.
- It's off to school with a breakfast bar!

Battle Plan! Courage. This time, after her daughter blows up, Mom leaves the room in less than ten seconds, saying nothing. That's the check-out. Can she consequence the behavior? Not really, there's no time. Remaining calm and quiet, Mom picks up her daughter and carries her out to the car. The girl screams half way to school then quiets down. Mom hands her a breakfast bar—still saying nothing. Drop off, kiss goodbye, see you later. Episode should be forgotten and not discussed anymore.

To bed or not to bed? Anatomy

"Bedtime for my 29-month-old son is horrible. Routines don't help. If I hear the "make sure you have a routine" diatribe again I'll go crazy. We still keep a steady routine of Bath, Brush, Bed and Books, but he still throws a fit ◀ **Explosion (protest)** *every night when we try to leave the room. The worst part is that every night he throws* **Veto** *a fit I get frustrated... my wife gets frustrated with me... and we end up mad at each other.* **HELP!"**

Weak

– Frustrated Father

In our next example it's the parents who are, in effect, requesting that their two-and-a-half-year-old go to bed. They cannot give the child what he wants, which might be to stay up all night or sleep with them. So they do a weak version of finalizing the Veto when they anxiously leave the room—with the child still in it. All hell breaks loose, partly because the boy doesn't want to be left alone and partly because he senses their worry (about a blowup) and their mixed feelings. Sure the parents have their routine of books, bed, bath and so on, but what don't they have a routine for? The kid's meltdown!

Bedtime What to do

- **Cause of tantrum:** child does not want activity
- **Can parents give child what he wants?** No.
- **Veto:** "Good night." Leave room.
- **Child files protest/explodes:** Throws fit.
- **Parents are already checked out!** Stay that way.
- **Consequence the behavior?** No.
- Use "cut them off at the pass" routine.

Here we give these parents a routine for the tantrum. With calm, courage and resolve Mom and Dad say "Good night" and they walk straight out of the room. Then, like with our little lollipop girl, this toddler's protest and explosion happen immediately. Can the parents check out? Yes, in fact, they are already checked out! No need for the 10-Second Rule here. They stay disengaged: no eye contact, talk or going back in the room. Can they consequence the tantrum? No, because it's bedtime and the boy is already in bed. If these parents feel the child may be a bit fearful, they can use the "cut them off at the pass" routine (*1-2-3 Magic*): Sit in the doorway, back to the room, and read until the child goes to sleep.

Angry Birds Anatomy

"Can I play Angry Birds on your iPad?"
"No, dear."
"Why not?"   Veto
"We're eating in ten minutes."

"Oh, come on. Just for five minutes."
"Read my lips. I said 'No'!"   Incubation
"You never let me do anything!"
"What!? We just got back from the pool!"

"That's stupid! I hate you!!"   Explosion

Here's our third example. Request Time: This kid's desire is to play Angry Birds for ten minutes before dinner. Could the parents grant that wish? Sure. If they did, there would be no problem. Everybody would be happy. But let's say they don't want to for whatever reason. They "finalize" the Veto with "No dear" and one explanation, "We're eating in ten minutes."

So far, so good. But the boy files a protest with "Oh, come on." The parent then blows her finalization of the Veto to smithereens with "Read my lips..." and so on. This ridiculous conversation is a classic case of tantrum incubation and it leads directly to the youngster's blowup.

Angry Birds What to do

OK. Take 2 for the Angry Birds incident. The parents were doing all right until the boy filed his protest. So after his "Oh, come on. Just for five minutes," they should disengage right away (which is less than 10 seconds) and say nothing. They already have stated their case and given an explanation. If the boy drops the issue, fine. If he decides to harass them further, they can maintain their silence, leave the room, or consequence his behavior.

- **Cause of tantrum:** child wants activity
- **Can parent give child what he wants?** Yes or no.
- **Veto:** "We're eating in ten minutes."
- **Child files protest:** "Oh, come on. Just for five minutes."
- **Parent checks out immediately.** Silence.
- **If child pushes further, consequence the behavior.**

Asking for Trouble!

Talking after a child's protest is filed or after the kid melts down is a surefire way to cut your own throat. What's the youngster supposed to say, "Gee, I never looked at it like that before" and then give up his request? "Trying to reason further after a protest/explosion will almost surely lead to the B.A.D. Syndrome and to the child's either getting his way or getting effective revenge.

The bottom line in preventing or managing meltdowns? Put your thinking cap on when Request Time arrives. Give the kids what they want if you can. If not, finalize the Veto quickly, then keep quiet and prepare for disengagement if they file a protest. Maintain your disengagement until calm is restored, but be prepared to consequence their behavior if you feel that is necessary.

What about the noise?

As mentioned earlier, one of the hardest parts of a tantrum for parents to put up with is the sound of the meltdown: *the noise!* When you

have to check out, it's best if you wait for the tantrum to subside on its own without any intervention from you. But the noise can stimulate that combination of rage and panic (temporary insanity) that 1) is very hard to listen to and 2) can become dangerous by raising the threat of physical child abuse.

Don't feel shy about using noise reduction devices, such as headphones, loud music or even TV. Ear plugs can also be helpful. It also will help if the kids know you can't hear all or most of their yelling. For safety reasons, you may want to hear just enough to know when peace has been restored.

If you like flow charts, here's a nice flow chart summary of Lesson II. Adapt this Battle Plan to your situation and then memorize it! You will prevent about half of the tantrums with steps 1 and 2. With steps 3 and 4 you will be prepared to respond to either protests or melt-downs within 10 seconds. Most of the time mild protests should be ignored and not consequenced.

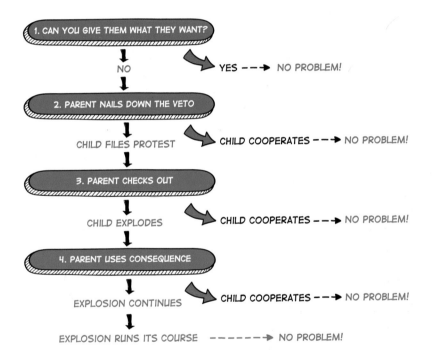

1. CAN YOU GIVE THEM WHAT THEY WANT?

NO   YES – – ➔ NO PROBLEM!

2. PARENT NAILS DOWN THE VETO

CHILD FILES PROTEST   CHILD COOPERATES – – ➔ NO PROBLEM!

3. PARENT CHECKS OUT

CHILD EXPLODES   CHILD COOPERATES – – ➔ NO PROBLEM!

4. PARENT USES CONSEQUENCE

EXPLOSION CONTINUES   CHILD COOPERATES – – ➔ NO PROBLEM!

EXPLOSION RUNS ITS COURSE   – – – – – ➔ NO PROBLEM!

Let's Get This Right!

A SUMMARY OF LESSON II

You have Vetoed a child's request for something.
Look away from the youngster, remain silent or
leave the area.

Stay flexible and relaxed, but be prepared for a protest or
explosion. If that's what you get, you'll have ten seconds
to react appropriately.

Minor protests may sound like this:

Minor protests should be quietly ignored. Reacting with irritation or anger makes you look guilty and vulnerable. This encourages more complaints from your kids.

If the child is safe, many explosions can simply be ignored.
Be quiet. Go somewhere else if possible
until the outburst is over.

You may want to escort a young child—or send an older
child—to their room to finish the meltdown. Usually it's a
bad idea to discuss the matter later.

Why do you check out after a protest or explosion? Because at this time you are three potential things to your kid:

You are the target of their anger.

You are the audience for their tantrum.

You have the power to give them what they want.

By withdrawing or disengaging, you allow your youngster to work out their frustration on their own rather than taking revenge out on you, trying to make you feel sorry for them, or continuing to try to get what they want.

These are the sounds of parental whimpering:

Answer this question:
What probable effects will these adult comments
have on the kids' tantrums?

Handle meltdowns well.
Learn to forgive your child and yourself for whatever happened.
Then go on with your life.

Repeat as necessary.

Lesson 3: What If?

Chapter 7

FAQs: Troubleshooting

So now you've got your new toolkit for managing meltdowns. In it are drastic new ways of thinking about the problem as well as drastic new ways of handling the problem. You also appreciate the fact that you have only ten seconds—after your child protests about not getting what they want—to make up your mind. The more seconds you spend in the B.A.D. Syndrome, the more you inadvertently reinforce your kid's chances of either getting what they want or, at least, getting effective revenge.

You have not seen your child's last tantrum

Even with your new tools, you still must reluctantly admit that *your child or children will tantrum again* at some point. The good news about that is that you will be much more ready for them when they do meltdown. You'll get a chance to practice—in real battle—your new ideas and tactics. The bad news is that there is an unknown here: How will your youngsters react to your new behavior? We don't know for sure.

Eliminating the B.A.D. Syndrome means answering all "What ifs?" in advance

Even though we don't know for sure how your kids will respond, we can say two things: 1) We can make some pretty good guesses as to what your kids will do, and 2) It is very important that we make our best predictions about the kids' future behavior. Good predictions will increase your confidence.

How can we make some educated guesses about your children's reactions to your new tactics? For one thing, you know your kids well. That means you can guess well. For another thing, kids only have so many options. In *1-2-3 Magic*, for example, there are only Six Kinds of Testing and Manipulation. You can probably predict which ones are your kids favorites, and which ones they're likely to use on you once you start managing meltdowns differently.

Why is it important for us to predict the children's reactions to your new behavior? Because it will help you stay out of the B.A.D. Syndrome. The more you are worried about the kids overwhelming or outsmarting or outmaneuvering you, the less confident you will be (and appear) when trying to deal with them. Your anxiety will show, and the kid's behavior is then likely to get worse.

Dealing with the tantrum
NOW
Setting a precedent for the
FUTURE

You are also probably aware that anytime you manage a meltdown, you are not only managing the now, but you are also setting a precedent for the future. And *your kids remember these precedents!* Into their memory banks goes this information: "If I behave like this, this is what my mom or dad or grandma is likely to do. Is that worth it?" Sure, some kids will shape up relatively quickly, but others will take much longer—especially those children who have had lots and lots of experience triggering B.A.D. Syndromes in their adult caretakers.

What if?

So here are some of the questions that might be going through your mind. You may have others that we didn't think of. But at this point, it's important to try to anticipate—as much as we can—the troubles you may have with your kids' reactions to the new system. It's hard to think clearly in the midst of a child's tantrum. But anticipatory troubleshooting will increase your confidence. Increased confidence will decrease B.A.D. And decreased B.A.D. will help your kids shape up much more quickly.

What if they have a tantrum?

This is the basic problem, isn't it? You're afraid of your kid's blowing up. OK, scrap that attitude. Your child is going to have more meltdowns. You are going to think hard and firm up your resolve. Drastic change #1 is accepting the fact of tantrums and preparing for them. Nail down that Veto quickly. No, they can't have what they want right now. Stop talking and let them do what they do. If they explode, disengage within ten seconds. That's drastic change #2. Ride out the tantrum and consequence their behavior if you want to. Give yourself a pat on the back if you earned it, but hold yourself to a high, new and precise standard when it comes to handling meltdowns.

What if they keep pleading or follow me around screaming?

This is a frequent question from parents. What if the kids won't shut up and they go wherever I go and continue complaining? Well, what's the first thing to remember? *You can't talk.* Talk—even angry talk from you—is putting gas on the fire. Second, how can you intensify or improve on your check-out or withdrawal? With a younger child, lock yourself in the bathroom. Or put them in a Pack 'n Play or in their room with a gate on the door. With an older boy or girl, set up an understanding that for every minute they bug you, they will lose so much off their allowance, or bedtime will be that much earlier. Just point to your watch to activate that deal. If worse comes to worse, just sit in the kitchen and cry. But no "dialogue"!

What if they yell in the car?

You're trapped in the car. The kid is mad as all get-out. At least they're stuck in their seat belt! Once again, you may not talk in the sense of dialogue or persuasion. If you need to, you may say, "We'll pull over 'til you're quiet." But nothing else. If you have to get where you're going, you can use counting from *1-2-3 Magic* and then come up with a consequence. Or crank up the music. Remember: Your arguing or persuading or whatever makes the meltdown worse, and that makes you a more dangerous driver. Think of all the accidents that have occurred because tantruming kids upset and distracted their parents. How many innocent folks have been killed like that?

- **Disengage totally.**
- **Pull off to side of road until they're quiet.**
- **Count.**
- **Crank up the music.**

What if they break things or wreck their room?

If you're going to use a bedroom for a rest period (time-out) or simply as a form of disengagement, remove any valuable or dangerous items in advance if you think the child may break them or get violent with them. If  the kid has a hammer and a saw in his room, for example, get those things out of there. If a child wrecks his or her room (some will!), be ready. Older kids will pay for items destroyed. Both older and younger kids will also have to live in the mess they create until they're over this initial testing period. If you are concerned about your personal safety or the safety of other family members, consider asking a neighbor, relative or even the police to help out. Police do this kind of thing a lot—but no crying wolf!

- Older kids pay for items broken.
- Don't clean up the room.
- Remove valuable or dangerous items.
- With bigger kids consider using the police when safety is an issue (assault, property damage).

What if they want to negotiate?

This question can be a little tricky, but not if you really think hard and think clearly. If a request is hanging in the air (from you or from a child), you can certainly talk things over. If the kids then get what they want, there will be no problem. But if you do not grant their wish, say what you need to quickly and then keep quiet. Don't expect them to thank you for not granting their desire. Negotiation after a Veto is final is not negotiation any more. It's Incubation! Disengage and consider counting (if you know *1-2-3 Magic*) or using a consequence if necessary.

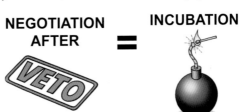

NEGOTIATION AFTER **VETO** **=** **INCUBATION**

What if **I just try to avoid the Veto?**

This is a tactic some parents have used with success, while in other families it just makes matters worse. The tactic is to avoid answering the child's request. After a request, for example, some parents say, "Wait here" while they then go to the bathroom or make a phone call. They hope the child will forget about whatever it was they wanted. Other parents say, "Maybe later, but if you bug me about it the answer is no." Personal research may be required in your home before you know whether or not avoiding the Veto is a viable option. If it doesn't work, you have 10 seconds to recover and decide on your next move! It will not be reasoning, pleading or whimpering.

What if **they won't go to rest period?**

You may want to use a rest period, break time or time-out strategy either for disengagement or as a consequence. If the child refuses to go, *you may not try to verbally persuade* them to go. With little kids, just move toward them. Many will then go. Otherwise, you may escort or even carry them to the room. With the older kids, the understanding is if they don't go, there will be a rest-period alternative. Fines, groundings from electronic gadgets, chores and community service can all be considered. What if they just follow you around jabbering angrily? Oops, we already answered that question!

What if **they won't stay in the rest period?**

If a child is angry enough to be melting down, he probably is not going to stay put on a time-out chair or stair. Some will, but most won't. For little kids, then, secure the door with a gate, Dutch door, plastic doorknob cover or some other method you are comfortable with. For older kids, use a time-out alternative as we discussed in the last question.

We saved the biggest "What if?" question for last.

Chapter 8

Out in Public

This is the ultimate meltdown-related question from parents. What on earth am I supposed to do when my youngster throws a huge tantrum right in the middle of the grocery store? What do I do when I feel all eyes are on me, and when my little one feels like he has the world's largest audience to play up to?

Two big concerns

We asked parents what their biggest fears were in these public situations. They mentioned two things.

1. Public embarrassment

2. Getting reported to DCFS

Certainly the embarrassment of looking like a rotten parent in front of millions of people is a big deal. Experiencing both panic and rage—as well as the full B.A.D. Syndrome—with an audience is a horrible thought. But the other thing parents worried about was the possibility of getting reported to their local version of child protection services and the possibility of an investigation and its consequences.

Remember: Kids can smell your resolve

So let's answer these questions. What are you going to do in public? How are you going to not get reported? How are you going to keep up your resolve with what feels like a potentially hostile audience? The answer is fairly simple, but it's not fairly easy. First, you are going to up your courage and up your resolve to steel-like proportions. Then? You're going to do much the same thing you would do if no one were watching! Let's work through an example.

Imagine this scene...

You're at a July 4th barbecue at a friend's house. Over thirty adults and kids are present. The hamburgers and hot dogs are on the grill and you're all going to eat in about half an hour. Your six-year-old son sees a plate of chocolate chip cookies on a wooden table in the yard. He asks you if he can have one. Since it's so close to lunch, you say no. He asks, "Why not?" You say, "Cause we're eating lunch in twenty minutes." He says, "Please, just one?" You reply, "Don't bug me!" and he blows up, screaming and yelling at you right in front of everyone. What are you going to do? Let's put this situation through our four step Battle Plan.

Remember our flow chart!

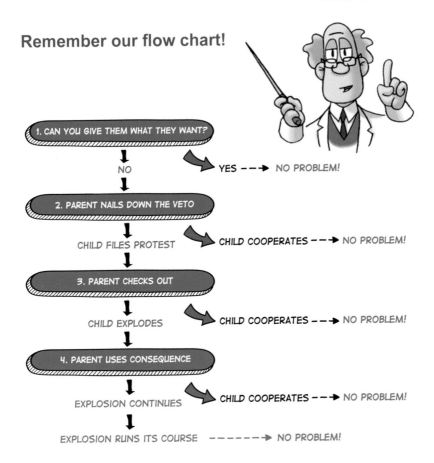

1. CAN YOU GIVE THEM WHAT THEY WANT?

NO   YES - - → NO PROBLEM!

2. PARENT NAILS DOWN THE VETO

CHILD FILES PROTEST   CHILD COOPERATES - - → NO PROBLEM!

3. PARENT CHECKS OUT

CHILD EXPLODES   CHILD COOPERATES - - → NO PROBLEM!

4. PARENT USES CONSEQUENCE

EXPLOSION CONTINUES   CHILD COOPERATES - - → NO PROBLEM!

EXPLOSION RUNS ITS COURSE   - - - - - → NO PROBLEM!

1. **Could you have given the boy what he asked for?** Certainly. It's a special occasion (and you would mention that fact if you decided to give him the cookie). Or you could have done something creative, such as this: "Pick a cookie and we'll give you a small part of it now. After lunch, you can finish this cookie and also have another." Chances are there would be no problem with either of these alternatives. But what if you didn't want to let him have the dessert before the lunch? It's on to the next step.

2. **No one else is paying much attention to the two of you. Yet!** You are going to quickly and firmly nail down the Veto: **"You can't have one before lunch. You can have one after lunch."** Now is the time for you to start being decisive and courageous. You know your son can melt down in public, but after you have explained once, do not allow your anxiety to goad you into useless pleading or whimpering. Pleading is a great way to START or trigger a meltdown. So when he says, "Please," you turn around and walk away.

 "Please" is his filing of a protest. You are going to gently disengage. If he wants to tantrum in front of everyone, he can do it by himself. Maybe everyone will forget whose kid he is! A crisp Veto and a quick withdrawal will abort many meltdowns. So you breathe a sigh of relief and go somewhere else to find someone to talk to.

But what if you son explodes AND decides to follow you around yelling at you—in front of everyone? Within ten seconds you decide to go back to your car, for a walk down the sidewalk, off to a corner of your friend's yard, or wherever. You do not talk to your son or make eye contact. He may find this more aggravating and yell louder. You maintain disengagement and get as far away from the party as possible.

 What's next? Consequence if you need to. Say once to your son, "We'll go back when you're done screaming." Nothing else. Or, if your son initially wanted to go to the party, you might say, "If you're not quiet in two minutes, we're going home." Or, "I'm timing you. For each minute you tantrum, you'll lose 25 cents off your allowance." Then you quietly wait for him to decide what to do.

Recall the grocery store scene...

What if you're in public but you don't have as much geographical flexibility as you did in the last scene? This kid wants a candy bar in the grocery store check-out line. You said no. Bam! He's off to the races, screaming and yelling. Three people behind you, clerk has already started ringing up your stuff. Maybe you could have given the kid a candy bar, but you didn't want to.

You're caught and *you feel like an idiot, but you can still handle the situation well*. You think, "Tantrums are a normal reaction to good parenting." After saying, "No candy today," you say nothing—unless it is to talk to the cashier. You check out from your son in the check-out line. Sure you want to scream at him or worse. Maybe you push the cart ahead a little, turn it around so the boy's as far from everyone as possible, and unload quickly. Maybe you apologize to the other folks, but you say nothing to your son.

Can you consequence the child? Not in this situation. You take him out to the car and put him in his car seat. You continue your disengagement and crank up the music on the way home. After he's quiet, you relax and restrain your desire to get back at him. It's life as usual after you get home. Your son will get over the incident long before you will. It's all part of being a parent. What a job!

How to not get reported to DCFS

1. Look like you know what you're doing

- **Be calm and decisive**
- **Act like you've been there before.**

2. Know what you're doing!

- **10-Second Battle Plan**
- **No B.A.D. Syndrome**

By now you should be getting a feel for the drill. So what if you're afraid of getting reported to your local child protection agency? Remember, it's not what your kid does that will get you reported, it's what you do.

First, *look like you know what you're doing*. If it's request time and there's the danger of a meltdown, remind yourself that meltdowns are normal and not the end of the world. Think prevention first. If possible, give the kid what she wants or, if you can't, nail down the Veto quickly and stop talking. Let the youngster be free to respond however she wants.

Second, *really know what you're doing*. This isn't your first tantrum to manage and it won't be your last. Be ready with your 10-Second Battle Plan if the child files a protest or blows up. Do a thorough job of gentle disengagement! Enjoy it if you can. No B.A.D. whimpering. Consequence if necessary.

Now imagine your child's most frequent tantrum

What's the situation? What's the request usually? If we had a video of you at that moment, how much B.A.D. would we see in your face and voice and behavior? Do you whimper a lot? How about angry chatter?

Now let's change that. Drastic change #1: What are you going to THINK differently? Lots of parents think this: "Tantrums are normal and I (parent) did nothing wrong." But managing the meltdown is your job—no one else's.

Next is drastic change #2: Calm disengagement. Sure it's not what you feel like doing. Too bad. HOW are you going to do it and how long can you keep it up? How long will it take your kids to realize that there's new management in town?

Let's Get This Right!

A SUMMARY OF LESSON III

This Mom is having a "What if?" thought.
Her thought is this: "What if my son has a meltdown?"

If this Mom can't answer her "What if?" thought,
she is setting herself up for the

This parent has answered all his "What if?" thoughts regarding the possibility of his youngster having a huge tantrum.

This dad knows what he is going to do next time. He knows there will be a next time. He understands the 10-Second Rule.

These are three of our Facebook
posts from the introduction:

Lately, his tantrums make me feel like I've failed, especially in public as I have a very defiant, over-reactive, loud 5-year-old who I've got no way to connect with once he gets in that mood. Vanessa R.

What can you say to Vanessa?

My little boy's meltdowns do me in for the day. Ella J.

Give Ella some advice.

You cannot reason with a child that is already tantruming. Diane S.

Do you agree with Diane? Why or why not?

Another fun outing:

Tell these parents
A) What to think and
B) What to do.

Right now!

Adult whimpering in public causes …

How are you going to avoid the B.A.D. Syndrome
when you're out and about with the kids?

Are You Ready?

On page 14 we mentioned that for this program to work we needed two things from you. You would need to be both

1. **Supportive of yourself:**
   Kind and sympathetic—
   tantrums are a tough problem!

2. **Demanding of yourself:**
   Master basic concepts and do
   the job well.

Well now it's time for the demanding part. Let's see how well you understand what you just read. On the next five pages are 20 multiple choice questions. There is only one correct answer for each question. The answers are on pages 88–90. It is our opinion that you will be ready to start and implement this program when you can answer 75% of these questions correctly.

If you get a question wrong, you will see the page you can refer to find the right answer. Hopefully you'll soon be on your way. The kids will never know what hit 'em! Good luck!

Final Exam

1. **What % of 4-year-olds have tantrums daily?**
    A. 100%
    B. 50%
    C. 11%
    D. 0%

2. **In the B.A.D. Syndrome, what does the "D" stand for?**
    A. Dumbfounded
    B. De fault is not mine
    C. Distracted
    D Default to reasoning

3. **What effect does a parent's B.A.D. state of mind have on a child's meltdown?**
    A. Makes it worse
    B. Makes it better
    C. Makes it stop
    D. Has no effect

4. **Why are parental Vetoes basically good things?**
    A. Because kids can act like brats sometimes
    B. Because parents should give children what they want
    C. Because parents can't give kids everything they want
    D. Because parents often simply need a break

5. **Why do moms and dads need to be understanding of themselves while managing tantrums?**
    A. Because they're good people
    B. Because managing tantrums can be emotionally draining
    C. So they can remember what to do
    D. So their spouse/partner will cooperate

6. **Which is NOT a typical outcome of repeated tantrums from children?**

    A. Marital stress
    B. Maternal depression
    C. Physical abuse of children
    D. High self-esteem in parents

7. **Which item below is one of the three main causes of tantrums?**

    A. Not getting a thing
    B. Regular nightmares
    C. Having to attend school
    D. Electronic overload

8. **Kids who are melting down are usually**

    A. Totally out of control
    B. Extremely focused on their goal
    C. Unaware of what they are doing
    D. None of the above

9. **There's been a Veto and a child has blown up. It's important for a parent to remember**

    A. The parent did nothing wrong
    B. The child has done nothing wrong
    C. Both parent and child are misbehaving
    D. Distraction and reasoning are often useful

10. **The Incubation stage often involves**

    A. Angry silence
    B. A child who is indifferent
    C. A really ridiculous conversation
    D. High frustration tolerance on the child's part

11. Adult whimpering in a crisis

    A. Will usually silence a child's protest or meltdown

    B. Has no effect on a frustrated youngster

    C. Will usually aggravate a child's protest or meltdown

    D. Will drive away most kids

12. We would like our children to learn

    A. Low frustration tolerance

    B. High frustration tolerance

    C. Medium frustration tolerance

    D. Frustration tolerance is an irrelevant concept in
       child discipline

13. The 10-Second Rule means you have only ten seconds to decide what to do after

    A. A child has gone to bed

    B. You have given a short lecture

    C. You realize that a request is coming

    D. A child has filed a protest or exploded

14. Distraction and reasoning after a protest or meltdown has occurred

    A. Are never good ideas

    B. Are only good ideas if they work

    C. Distraction is OK but not reasoning

    D. Should be continued even if they don't work
       right away

15. Your two choices BEFORE a child files a protest or explodes are

    A. Nail down the Veto then negotiate

    B. Negotiate after a 15-minute break

    C. Ignore the child's request

    D. Give them what they want or nail down the Veto

16. Your two choices AFTER a child files a protest or explodes are
    A. Nail down the Veto then negotiate
    B. Check out then consequence if necessary
    C. Ignore the child's protest then argue
    D. Use the Talk, Persuade, Argue, Yell sequence

17. The three reasons you check out after a protest or explosion are
    A. You are the parent and it's your decision
    B. You are the audience, the power and the parent
    C. You have a right, a duty and a job
    D. You are the audience, the target and the power

18. Which is NOT a good tactic if a child is tantruming in the car
    A. Crank up the music
    B. Tell them in no uncertain terms to keep quiet
    C. Pull off to the side of the road
    D. Disengage totally

19. You can negotiate with the kids
    A. Only after the Veto has been finalized
    B. Only after a protest has been filed
    C. Only before the Veto has been finalized
    D. Never negotiate—it's your house

20. Parents' two biggest fears regarding public meltdowns were
    A. Not having enough time to finish shopping and public embarrassment
    B. Public embarrassment and their own anger
    C. Controlling their own anger and the cost of groceries
    D. Getting reported to DCFS and public embarrassment

Final Exam Answers

1. What % of 4-year-olds have tantrums daily?
   C. 11%
   Page 17

2. In the B.A.D. Syndrome, what does the "D" stand for?
   D. Default to reasoning
   Page 25

3. What effect does a parent's B.A.D. state of mind have on a child's meltdown?
   A. Makes it worse
   Page 26

4. Why are parental Vetoes basically good things?
   C. Because parents can't give kids everything they want
   Page 33

5. Why do moms and dads need to be understanding of themselves while managing tantrums?
   B. Because managing tantrums can be emotionally draining
   Page 14

6. Which is NOT a typical outcome of repeated tantrums from children?
   D. High self-esteem in parents
   Pager 12

7. Which item below is one of the three main causes of tantrums?
   A. Not getting a thing
   Page 17

8. Kids who are melting down are usually

   B. Extremely focused on their goal
   Page 18

9. There's been a Veto and a child has blown up.
   It's important for a parent to remember

   A. The parent did nothing wrong
   Pages 17-19

10. The Incubation stage often involves

    C. A really ridiculous conversation
    Pages 22-23

11. Adult whimpering in a crisis

    C. Will usually aggravate a child's protest or meltdown
    Page 26

12. We would like our children to learn

    B. High frustration tolerance
    Page 27

13. The 10-Second Rule means you have only ten seconds to
    decide what to do after

    D. A child has filed a protest or exploded
    Page 28

14. Distraction and reasoning after a protest or meltdown
    has occurred

    B. Are only good ideas if they work
    Page 38

15. Your two choices BEFORE a child files a protest or explodes are

    D. Give them what they want or nail down the Veto
    Page 42–44

16. Your two choices AFTER a child files a protest or explodes are

    B. Check out then consequence if necessary
    Page 45-47

17. The three reasons you check out after a protest or explosion are

    D. You are the audience, the target and the power
    Page 46, 61

18. Which is NOT a good tactic if a child is tantruming in the car

    B. Yell at them in no uncertain terms to keep quiet
    Page 68

19. You can negotiate with the kids

    C. Only before the Veto has been finalized
    Page 69

20. Parents' two biggest fears regarding public meltdowns were

    D. Getting reported to DCFS and public embarrassment
    Page 71

Go Get 'em!

MELTDOWNS

Have you had enough?

Don't play the game out of

FEAR

Don't play the game out of

ANGER

Play it
SMART!

What to Expect:

1. Give 'em what they want.   25%

2. Lock down your Vetoes.   25%

3. Gently Check Out.   25%

4. Consequence if necessary.   25%

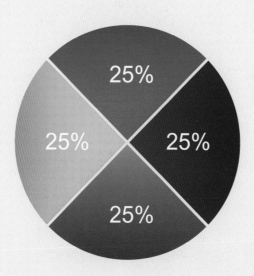

Though this will vary some from family to family,
each of our four strategies should reduce the total
volume of tantrums by about 25%.

Good Luck!